D1143255

On Freedom

Celebrating ten years of
Belarus Free Theatre

On Freedom

Powerful polemics by supporters of

Belarus Free Theatre

Foreword by
TOM STOPPARD

Edited by
FENELLA DAWNAY

OBERON BOOKS
LONDON

WWW.OBERONBOOKS.COM

CONTENTS

FOREWORD

To take a parochial view at a given moment – the view from what we call the Western world after what we call the Enlightenment – the conversation about freedom, both as a concept and a practical issue, became immensely more complicated as the twentieth century bled into the twenty-first. I came to freedom late. I was in my twenties before I stopped taking freedom for granted, and in my thirties before I began writing about it. The subject did not seem particularly complicated to me: it hinged tidily on the Iron Curtain. (Is that phrase still familiar to anyone born after the collapse of Soviet Communism?) I lived in the Free World, where abuses were failures of the system, and I wrote – occasionally – about the totalitarian world where abuses were the system in working order. Simple as it was, my idea of freedom was no simpler than the monolithic fact of the Iron Curtain as manifested by the Berlin Wall. I was fond of observing that a child could see that a utopia which stopped people leaving was a prison; which was true, of course, but how quaint, how simplified, that world view seems now when razor wire is putting up new barriers overnight in the path of refugees from dystopias more frightful than anything conceived by the tyrant acolytes of Marx or Mao; when one must span history and geography, to the Middle Ages, to Pol Pot, in seeking a comparison; when one's enemy's enemy is one's enemy.

And yet, beneath the confusion (we have to believe this) the necessity of freedom, autonomous freedom, the freedom of the individual, is an innate, unerasable condition of the wholly lived life, and that condition holds true on every scale. The rights of the individual underpin the rights of populations. It is the same right. If, in the face of huge collective enormities, we sideline what seems relatively slight in scale and acuteness, we break the connection between 'rights' and rightness.

This book appears under the auspices of a theatre group which makes that connection in the work it has been creating in exile from its homeland, an anachronistic dictatorship in a Europe which has become a present-day Promised Land, as another land was for the persecuted of another time and another place. We can't compare the denying of what we venerate as the freedoms of a modern secular society with the despotism of theocracies, still less with the barbarism which kills and displaces millions. But nor do we need to. A war in defence of civilised values is unintelligible without the consciousness of our ideals. This book speaks for those.

Tom Stoppard is a playwright and screenwriter. He first met Belarus Free Theatre in 2005.

We like to consider freedom as an ultimate good and treat its protection and enjoyment as the mark of an open society. But we also fear it. That tension and contradiction is repeatedly played out in our ambivalence towards freedom of speech.

It is a relative right whose limits are never clear and is the first to fall victim to constraints at times of national crisis or moral outrage. It is therefore at once the most precious and vulnerable of rights, and its protection requires constant vigilance.

The contradiction in our attitude towards free speech was evident to the world after the shocking Charlie Hebdo murders. Politicians marched on the streets of Paris, desperate to identify themselves with 'Charlie' and join in an unprecedented moment of global support for free speech. But within days, the French police were arresting individuals who made provocative statements about the murders for 'glorifying' terrorism, while the British government was busy introducing legislation to curb extremism that would undermine the freedom of universities and schools to enjoy free speech and unconstrained debate.

At a time of heightened fear of terrorism, the immediate instinct of politicians is to control and ban speech. Yet this censorship actually undermines the very values they are seeking to protect: the freedom to explore ideas, dissent from the mainstream and challenge orthodoxy is the lifeblood of democracy, creativity and individuality. It's not a freedom we should ever sacrifice for some purported higher cause.

Since the publication of *The Satanic Verses* twenty-seven years ago, the trend towards censorship has become an established and much repeated response to speech that offends. The emergence of the idea that avoiding offence may be more important than defending the right to free speech has dangerously undermined our protection of freedom of expression.

Now that the UK government is pushing through further legislation to tackle extremism that will further curb our freedom – our academic, cultural and political freedom – it has never been more necessary to fight for its defence.

Jo Glanville is director of English PEN, an organisation that campaigns to defend freedom of expression.
She is a longtime supporter and fan of Belarus Free Theatre.

I did not think about freedom until my husband disappeared. Even then, I was not concerned about my personal freedom. In my grief and during the long search for the truth I started to think about freedom as an essential component of human rights, justice and democracy.

For most of my life I lived a normal life in what I thought was a normal country, Belarus. I was born in a small town, made a good career as a University professor, had a loving husband, good kids and a nice apartment, which was a big deal in the Soviet Union. I was happy where I was, starting with nothing and having more than any of my relatives had ever achieved. Yes, I could compare my life only with the lives of people around me. Information about other worlds was completely restricted. But we could read clever books, and we had brains. And in the beginning of the 1990s we got a great gulp of freedom. We understood it immediately and enjoyed it so much. We participated in street demonstrations against the old political system.

We joked in public about the illiteracy and stupidity of the new president and we started to campaign for the return of the Belarusian language which had been abandoned during the Soviet period. We thought that freedom had been granted to us and that we would have it forever. But then everything stopped. My husband and other politicians disappeared. My friends were put in prison. And freedom died.

During sixteen years of seeking justice for my husband and my friends, I realized that to achieve this aim I would first have to seek freedom for my country, which had been destroyed by more than twenty years of dictatorship.

Today freedom for me is to live in my own country and not to be afraid that one day another loved one will disappear because his or her opinion is different from those who rule.

Freedom for me is when those who are responsible for these crimes can be prosecuted in spite of their high official state position.

Freedom for me is when the government has the courage to apologize to the families of the disappeared and to establish the rule of law so that these crimes will not happen again.

Freedom for me is when I can finally find the grave of my husband, place flowers on his grave and say: 'Forgive us, please.'

Today, freedom for me means being able to live in the country where I was born and not be ashamed of what is going on there. Freedom will only be real when I see Belarus free of lies, intolerance and propaganda. Free of the dictator and the dictatorship.

Irina Krasovskaya is the President of the We Remember Foundation, which seeks justice for political disappeared in Belarus and worldwide. After the disappearance of her husband, Irina spent time with Natalia Kaliada and Nicolai Khalezin talking about justice, life, and love. These conversations became the basis of the play *Discover Love* that remains in Belarus Free Theatre's repertoire.

Perfect freedom doesn't exist. The freedom we talk and dream about is only in our heads. The limitation is us: our bodies, our houses, our relatives and close ones. This social life, which we are part of. We are dependent on these things, and that isn't bad! While we are here on Earth, freedom is inside ourselves. We are our own limitations of freedom.

Because we dream of freedom, we become driven by it and become hunters where the prey is our own dream, never to be satisfied.

If only you'd wait for a bit, you'd have everything, you'd have your freedom. This is why others let go of their worries and look forward, developing themselves and their search for freedom. Sometimes they find it, just for a moment, like a flash, and then they are calm and happy.

There is only one possible resolution and it is the same for everyone; the end of this life and the beginning of something new. No one knows what this something new is, because those who leave never come back. They have broken through their limitations. And this is the only way to obtain ideal freedom.

Yana Rusakevich joined Belarus Free Theatre in 2005. She was dismissed from the Yanka Kupala National Academic Theatre for co-operation with Belarus Free Theatre and has been arrested twice for her professional activities and participation in peaceful political street rallies.

Justice and freedom are the leading lights of humanity. During our history freedom has entrenched itself as a natural right. But our history itself was the result of a long conflict against freedom.

There is no normal life, normal love, normal writing, normal painting, normal expression, normal death without freedom. Liberty leads the people, as Delacroix painted.

There can be no freedom if we censor ourselves, especially in totalitarian regimes or dictatorships.

In Camera (1976)

Many times I do
Sit with myself
I close every gap and every window
I check to be sure nothing can go out
That there is total secrecy
And I see spectre coming out of myself
To watch me

What is the essence of life? It is the freedom to see the beauty of things:

Life, Women, Books, Music, Poetry, Stories, Theatre, Thoughts, Work, Comradeship.

Without freedom there can be no enjoyment of life.

But many things seek to limit that freedom.

Power, capital punishment without justice or mercy, wars that serve the mechanisms of trade and money and excuse their crimes, extremism, savage ideologies and the remnants of our brutal history. So we suffer from a shortage of freedom when we face this conflict between conformity and plurality.

We will always be faced with the challenges of power and the influence of politics, the battle between church and state.

To be truly free in the first half of the 21st century we would have to abandon everything and go back to when we lived in caves, where there was no power and the dark and the light were separate. When there were only two places for man, outside in the day and inside at night; and man was free to create any god he needed.

Dr Nabeel Yasin is an academic, journalist, writer and poet who had to flee his homeland Iraq under Saddam Hussein's dictatorship because of his poem 'The Poet Satirizes the King'. Nabeel has contributed to Belarus Free Theatre's website, Ministry of Counterculture.

The state representative is wearing sandals and sunglasses, holding my file. It is an informal meeting. He's trying to be helpful and replies to my disagreement. 'Yes, sir, I know you've always declared your income but, you see, we've discovered there's this other law from 2003 that –' 'Wait a second. You just discovered a law that you didn't know even existed. And now you're asking me to pay four years' worth of retroactive penalties because of it?' 'As a citizen you're required to know all the laws.' 'Even the ones that obviously the state doesn't know about?' 'Yes. This is how it works. Now there might be a loophole. If you talk to your former employers and ask them to make it look like –' 'Are you now suggesting I should do something illegal?' 'I'm just saying, sir... This could be so much less complicated for everyone. I'm not the one deciding these things. Between me and you: you didn't know about it, we didn't know about it...' 'So why not have my former employers forge documents and pay tax twice? No, I'm contesting this 'law' of yours. We both know this 'law' is interpreted this way because our President wants to control the unfriendly press. Artists like me are just casualties. The nature of this law itself means double taxation, which is illegal. There's going to be a lawsuit –' 'I'm begging you sir. You know how long lawsuits take in this country. Meanwhile, we'll just take everything from you. And what happens if you lose by the end of it? C'mon, make it easy for everyone.' I'm not sure if this guy is actually waiting for a bribe or just trying to be helpful. In this country you never know. Just like you never know how to bribe doctors. So I walk away.

The tax man is right. Very soon my life takes a big turn. All my accounts are frozen. Now everything I earn has to go to the state, to cover the humongous debt on my name. How I manage to eat food or pay rent with all the money going to them, it's just my problem. So I get off the grid. I take triple the amount of work, just so I can pay both the state and my living expenses. I work under pseudonyms, cash only. I undersell. I compromise. I create work

I don't need to create. I don't have free time. I destroy relationships. I get depressed. As I slowly am covering my debt, my life and everything I create belongs to the state. I'm a slave.

Four years go by. One day, out of the blue, the sandal-sunglass man calls me again. 'Sir, we're so sorry. Turns out we were wrong. That law was flawed in the first place. Fiscal amnesty. No hard feelings, OK?'

No hard feelings. The man is right. Actually I'm one of the lucky ones. So many people have lost countless years or even died fighting unclear, unjust laws of a free country that failed to officially condemn its totalitarian past or pass a lustration law. Freedom is a helpful sunglass guy in sandals, trying to make it easy.

Peca Stefan is a nomad Romanian playwright living and writing about the magic absurdity of life. Peca met and worked with Belarus Free Theatre in Minsk, 2008 on *Eurepica. Challenge.*

There's a saying. 'The only way to deal with an unfree world is to become so absolutely free that your very existence is an act of rebellion'. To be Black and Gay is by default an act of rebellion. All the overwhelming forces of censure, respectability and the twin pillars of racism and homophobia conspire to push me further and further to the edge of invisibility. Freedom is only gained when confronted by shouting loud and making a rukus. White folks want you to be part of a narrative of oppression, straight folks want a narrative of normality and Black folks want us to be their kind of essentialist Black.

So do I feel free and equal given the West's celebrated liberal legislation for Gay LGBT people and anti-racist laws? No I feel endangered and under siege, I feel restricted by a mainstream reductive idea of identity and lifestyle that seeks to police my love, desire and aspirations. Everything is cool in private but as soon as I step into the street I only have to hold my Black lover's hand or look at the police the wrong way or drive while Black, or walk down the wrong road wearing a hoodie and BAM! It's over for me. So I am forced to either be defiant or invisible.

Then there is the violence, the competitive behavior and the lack of vulnerability displayed by Black people, particularly men, to each other. This adds another layer of censure to how we can express our masculinity, difference and humanity. Social and cultural restrictions are backed up by a whole load of technology, surveillance cameras, automated number plate recognition, DNA sampling, racism in employment, the media, education and housing that further pressures me to either conform or find another way to head underground to remain out of sight: in the margins. Ultimately freedom, if you are Black and Gay, is gained at the price of stress on your mental health.

Moving forward, I think in the developed world we need a way of supporting subculture. The aggressive drive of capitalism and hetero-normative values including marriage and middle-class white aesthetics need to be challenged through strategic rethinking of what is valuable in a vibrant plural society.

We need to acknowledge that not everyone lives neat tidy lives and that the outsider is as important as the conformist in any vision of a civilized world. Being Black and Gay is a challenging intersection to human rights. Black queer people of colour are somebody's mother, father, brother, sister or tran relative. Not an abstract. Our lives impact on many families and individuals in countless ways and adds to the wider impact of inequality. This has to be addressed.

Topher Campbell is a writer, archivist, filmmaker and theatre director committed to making work that matters. He came in to contact with the work of Belarus Free Theatre at an inspiring human rights event at the House of Commons.

The issue of freedom is difficult for me. All my life I have lived in an undemocratic country and things that are unacceptable to some are usual for me. I guess freedom is the possibility to be yourself without limiting the freedoms of others. It is not having the feeling of someone constantly behind you, a presence you can't see. It is making your life your own. We are restricted by the mindset we inherit from our parents, which is why we have to accept people with different points of view and lifestyles. Then freedom is being unique amongst the unique.

Siarhei Kvachonak studied at the Belarusian State Technological University. In 2012 he was expelled from the University for his co-operation with Belarus Free Theatre.

I'm British. I don't have the freedom to libel folk, to outrage decency by causing harm and offence, I cannot discriminate on grounds of race or gender, I can't say things which give rise to public disorder...the list goes on. Those restrictions flow, if you like, from our values. But what are our freedoms? When rows erupt in the arts (whose job is to challenge and provoke) I always say that freedom of expression within the law is our most precious principle. So the question then is, are our laws liberal and humane?

For me the most important answer must be that our laws encourage plurality. They allow a BBC which is a state organisation to criticise the state. They fund the Arts Council to take informed, independent, 'arm's length' decisions on which works to invest in, whatever the content. We're not monocultural, monotheistic, monopolitical. That would not only be monotonous but totalitarian. The state and the law we look to for freedoms should encourage dissent, innovation, novelty.

When public money is invested in media and the arts it should demand greater risks than commercial money would. Today's outrage is tomorrow's mainstream. Freedom within liberal laws…drink it in: 'You don't know what you've got till it's gone.'

Sir Peter Bazalgette is Chair of Arts Council England. He was pleased to help organise a supporters' event for Belarus Free Theatre.

The most universal and compelling themes in all the Arts, has at its core what I call the **Liberation Narrative**. These are the stories we have been told as children, continue to tell to our children, tell our self, and tell each other that express a will and willingness to struggle for freedom.

Whether historical, symbolic, metaphoric, comical, ironic or tragic, these narratives are provocations and inspirations that serve to remind us that a life full of longing and pain, in triumph or defeat, is a journey worthy of every effort and every sacrifice.

Art, which makes vivid and meaningful the characters (our saints and our warlords, our demons and clowns) who have been woven into the fabric of our myths and lore, keeps us sensitive and empathetic to iniquity and injustice. Art keeps us focused on the individuals or systems that stifle and oppress us, whether as individuals or tribes, genders, communities or peoples, it is the art that continues to reset our moral compass.

It is to the **Liberation Narrative** we turn for the assurance that our struggles are authentic, shared and meaningful.

Eric Fischl is an American artist whose works are in the collections of museums around the world. He has been a supporter of Belarus Free Theatre since he was introduced to their work, their vision and their courage three years ago.

'It's terribly exhausting – to be free.'

– Theodore Zeldin

However many times you look in the dictionary to find the meaning of the word 'freedom', it won't bring you any closer to actually understanding what it means. Neither do the conflicting aphorisms of classic literature help to add any clarity. The deeper you get into the understanding of this concept, the more pointless the whole thing seems. For the past hundred years very few have managed to understand the true meaning of this word, and the names of those who have are now forever associated with the concept of freedom.

Jan Hus (1369–1415) was a Czech priest and a man who did not believe in religion for profit. He thought that no Pope or bishop had the right to take up the sword in the name of the Church, and that those who violated the Commandments of God should not be recognized as churchmen. This led the preacher to the fire, sentenced to be burnt to death at the stake, the sparks from which ignited a revolutionary movement and began the Hussite wars in Bohemia, a conflict which lasted for fifteen years. The controversial result of an indisputable truth. Forever tied to Hus' name are the actions of an old lady, who in her religious zeal planted a bundle of dried wood into the fledgling fire upon which the preacher was to burn. Crying out in pain Sancta Simplicitas! (translated as 'holy simplicity') he earned his posthumous aphorism, still used today to describe someone's stupid or naïve actions.

Giordano Bruno (1548–1600) was a Dominican monk and poet, who followed the teachings of Copernicus and made a number of conjectures about the structure of the solar system, stating that the stars were distant suns surrounded by their own planets, and that the universe was infinite, with no celestial body at its centre. His denial of core Catholic beliefs provoked a number of denunciations, which led to his arrest for the crime of heresy in 1592. Prison followed, eight years of torture and abuse, until he was sentenced to death by fire in

1600 at the Plaza of Flowers in Rome. 'To burn does not mean to deny,' he chanted several times before his death. Another aphorism gained by the history of free mankind, in exchange for a handful of ashes from a brave man. He left behind several works, which in 1600 were placed in the Catholic Index of forbidden books. In 1948 they were finally released to the general public, when even the most conservative members of the church understood that the Earth revolves around the Sun.

Aside from his work, which was significantly ahead of its time, what is most interesting about Giordano Bruno is that even 400 years after his death, in the year 2000, Cardinal Angelo Sodano referred to his execution merely as a 'sad episode', whilst commending the faithful actions of the Inquisition, who until the very end had tried to spare the life of the brave monk. So far the Roman Catholic Church has maintained that all Inquisition actions were faithful to the church. This position was held by Pope John Paul II, himself marked down in history as a man of freedom.

Vaclav Havel (1936–2011) a successful Czech literary critic and playwright, realised that socialism and communism are two types of utopia that inevitably lead to the collapse of society. We may never understand what, in 1975, drove this successful young man from a wealthy family to write an open letter to Gustav Husak, Head of the Communist Party of Czechoslovakia, warning of the imminent crisis to the country that Communism threatened. However tactfully and clearly expressed, the letter provoked Havel's arrest. Upon his release in 1978 he continuing his dissident activities, and was arrested again in 1979. Following his release due to poor health in 1983, he was arrested again in 1989. He contracted a whole set of respiratory diseases in prison, from which he suffered for the rest of his life, and which would eventually be the cause of his death.

'I favour politics as practical morality, as service to the truth, as essentially human and humanly measured care for our fellow humans.'[1] The words are those of a free man, one whose

---

1 Extract from Vaclav Havel's essay, 'Politics and Conscience', 1984.

political vision has not yet been accepted by the current political world.

When asked which politician most embodies the terms 'freedom' and 'conscience' the names that come up again and again are those of Vaclav Havel and Nelson Mandela.

Mandela was a supporter of non-violent resistance, a fighter against apartheid, an idol for generations of young people, a Nobel Peace Prize winner, he spent twenty-seven years in prison, arrested by the South African security forces on the advice of the American CIA. It is difficult to imagine enduring such a lengthy sentence. During those years artistic movements evolved, black-and-white television changed to colour, the Internet and mobile phones were developed, cures were found for diseases... Nelson Mandela spent those years in a 2x3m prison cell, his name taken from him and replaced with a number – 46664.

This talk on freedom is partially meaningless. It is a confusing term which defies comprehension – it's a contradiction that pairs the bad with the good, the good with the best, and the bad with the disgusting.

When we consider that word, we can be overwhelmed by the memory of those who lived by it and see a certain irony behind the idea: 'freedom is the absence of any restrictions'.

Nicolai Khalezin is a playwright, director, journalist and co-founding Artistic Director of Belarus Free Theatre. Nicolai is the author of eleven plays including *Generation Jeans* and *Here I Am* and has won numerous awards recognizing his contribution to humanitarian theatre. Nicolai is a founding member of Fortinbras, the only free theatre laboratory in Belarus, and the International Contest of Contemporary Drama, which he developed with Vladimir Shcherban and Natalia Kaliada.

DAVID LAN

You grow up looking at one particular tree outside your house. It's your tree. For you it is 'tree'. Your blue sky is 'sky'.

Later in life your tree, your sky appear in the songs you write or in your dreams. They're your place in the world and you can't think of them without being at some deepest level 'you'.

Some people find they're also deeply who they are in the shade of other people's trees, bathed in the light of other skies. They are the free.

David Lan is Artistic Director of the Young Vic theatre, where Belarus Free Theatre have been an associate company since 2011.

Liberté, Egalité, Fraternité. We are all for brotherhood and sisterhood, but the two greater human rights are Liberty and Equality. And of the two, which is the most important?

In the English tradition, liberty has always had the upper hand. The theory behind the free market and Adam Smith is that if we all have liberty then we can each make of our lives whatever we wish. It is, of course, a myth. 'All animals are equal,' pronounced Napoleon, in *Animal Farm*, 'but some animals are more equal than others.' One glance at the current Cabinet and anyone will understand that a person born with a silver spoon in his mouth tends to go to a Public School (which is actually private) where he is taught that liberty is the greatest right, and that if his spoon should metamorphose into gold, that is one of the glories of freedom. If Tristram Hunt should have attended such a school and (god forbid) tentatively suggests that some of their manifest inequalities should be pared back, he is tarred a hypocrite.

Liberty is of little use to someone who is starving. The freedom to get on a leaking and overcrowded boat to attempt a stormy crossing of the Mediterranean hardly guarantees happiness. Indeed, even the 'freedom' to purchase an ever increasing quantity of pointless items promoted by *Vogue* or *Maxim* magazine merely reflects the ugly cycle of consumerism.

Some years ago, there was a study in California that found three groups of people who tend to fit the classic definition of the sociopath – 'a person with a personality disorder manifesting itself in extreme antisocial attitudes and behaviour.' These groups were the doctor, the lawyer and the robber-murderer – as a vast generalisation, because the American doctor and lawyer generally join the profession in order to make money, rather than out of the milk of human kindness; and the robber-murderer chose the wrong parents and therefore did not have that option. Obviously many of the professionals do not fit this mould – I hope not, as I am an American lawyer. However, the capitalist with his 'liberty' untrammelled is a devastatingly selfish animal.

We do not need to read *The Spirit Level* to understand that a true, and perhaps gradual, focus on equality makes everyone happier. If we teach our children that they should always derive pleasure from helping those who are less fortunate, then everyone benefits – our child is happy, and the beneficiaries see their lives improved. If we reward those who seek to make our village a beautiful community, rather than those who seek to evict the tenants so that they can make more money from 'their' property, then everyone benefits.

Liberty is a significant right – ask anyone who has seen equality perverted in either a Soviet gulag or in *Animal Farm*. But with genuine equality, we have little fear of lost liberty, as everyone must protect your liberty to enjoy the same right.

Clive Stafford Smith is the director of the legal action charity Reprieve (reprieve.org.uk) and has been a supporter of, and occasional collaborator with, Belarus Free Theatre for several years.

Limitations on freedom can be very dangerous, because to create a civil society you need freedom of speech and we all know what happens in societies with just one source of information. I face this problem when my relatives, like zombies, believe the propaganda and lies of our politicians. It reminds me of the Nazis in Germany and how the German nation became enslaved by Goebbels' propaganda. But I hope we will not make the same mistakes again and that we will not let politicians or anyone who wants to limit our freedom fool us.

We must keep fighting for freedom. There are many ways to do it: be responsible; be conscious; fight your deepest fears. Don't be a bystander, fighting means action! As Stéphane Hessel said, 'To create is to resist, to resist is to create!'

Pavel Radak-Haradnitski joined Belarus Free Theatre in 2005. He is unable to apply for jobs in Belarus because of his association with Belarus Free Theatre and he has been detained for his professional activities.

'Freedom' is the second most popular word after 'love' in song lyrics. As with music, we need to free our minds and souls when it comes to our own personal, unofficial history. But before we can do this we need to free our hearts. Only by letting go of the fears, prejudices, historical disbeliefs and ideologies that we hold, can we free our souls. Of course this is a very optimistic way of thinking and the most difficult emancipation of humankind is to think that we can rid ourselves of the characteristics we carry, even in our chromosomes.

When I think of freedom I have a vision of a peaceful atmosphere in a beautiful pastoral scene. Maybe that is my own explanation of freedom: peace, serenity, silence, nature and calm. But when people inhabit my idea of freedom, then I begin to hear other voices, breathing, ideas, bodies. Then freedom becomes something more than an individual concept, it becomes a social phenomenon. Then peace slips from my vision. But if peace walks away can we still say we have freedom? For me peace is the ideal that should walk hand in hand with freedom.

When I think of today's societies all around the world, the idea of freedom differs, from the Middle East to Europe, from North Africa to South America. Even in Europe we have different terminologies and explanations for 'freedom'. There shouldn't be such a difference between the concept of freedom in England and Belarus. We are all human. We shouldn't have such different definitions of freedom in Berlin and in İstanbul. Unfortunately each nation has their own unique way of defining freedom according to the ideology of the State, systems of the government, religious traditions of the community or the democratic expectations of so-called 'modern citizens'. In today's world some countries are freer than others. But it only seems so. Perhaps we need a new definition of freedom. Unfortunately 'intolerance', 'nationalism', 'fascism', 'racial discrimination' and 'genocide' are still words that exist in all languages, and they are still in daily use.

None of us can be free while the corpses of Syrian refugees hit the Aegean shores of Turkey. None of us can be free until all the children on the verge of starvation in Africa are fed. We need a new set of humanist economic and political systems all over the world. Freedom comes with its best friend 'independence'. Nations should be independent of their economic welfares. Until that day we must find a new definition of freedom.

As Janis Joplin screamed once in 'Me and Bobby McGee': 'Freedom's just another word for nothing left to lose'

Özen Yula is a Turkish writer and director working internationally. He worked on *Eurepica. Challenge.* with Belarus Free Theatre

In the early summer of 2012 I drove to Minsk from a small town outside the Chernobyl exclusion zone. I met Andrei Sannikov there, the Presidential candidate who had been imprisoned in December 2010. Andrei, at that time, was under a curfew, and so was his wife, journalist Iryna Khalip. We sat at a kitchen table drinking Georgian wine and talking about their fading hope for democracy in Belarus.

I went on to a rehearsal at the Belarus Free Theatre. I knew Natalia Kaliada and Nikolai Khalezin from London – they had claimed asylum in Britain – and I was curious to see the original theatre. It was a tiny suburban house, two modest rooms thrown into one, an internal wall demolished with a sledgehammer. The young actors rehearsed. It was a dance of dictatorship, a dismal treading, a constant hum, and sudden, discordant, screams.

Is that the sound of dictatorships, I wondered – that dull tread around and around, that hum, those discordant screams. And if that is the sound of dictatorships, then what is the sound of freedom?

Almost the entire old city of Minsk was destroyed in the war. I looked at the broad socialist boulevards of the new city and thought of Le Corbusier's crazy plan to pull down and re-build a new and stream-lined Paris, or Ceauscescu's project of demented grandiosity; the destruction and re-building of old Bucharest. I wondered how a city can survive destruction of the kind Minsk endured – not just physical destruction, but also the deportations and deaths, war and occupation. I remembered reading that in 1926 over 40% of Minsk's population was Jewish. Most of them were murdered.

The actors showed me the remnant streets of old Minsk, and we talked about the free theatre, and their commitment to it. They seemed to me like any young actors in the West, or in Russia – they had mobile phones and western clothes and dyed hair. But they were taking a risk. It all seemed so normal, and yet I feared for them. Perhaps they feared for themselves. I don't know. Only two years earlier, Oleg Bebenin, the founder of Charter 97, and Sannikov's press secretary and friend was found hanged at his dascha. Many others had disappeared, amongst them Jury Zacharanka, the former Minister of Internal Affairs who had joined the opposition, Victor Gonchar, opposition politician, Anatol Krasouski, a businessman, and Dmitriy Zavadski, a cameraman. They are all presumed dead.

Since that trip the political freedom in many parts of the world has steadily declined. I try to remember when I was last optimistic about the world. A long time ago. Long before 9/11, before we had even heard of Guantanamo and torture memos. And before the genocides of Yugoslavia and Rwanda. A brief moment, around 1989. It seems a very long time ago.

Sigrid Rausing is the publisher and editor of Granta magazine, and the publisher of Granta Books and Portobello Books. She is a long-standing supporter of Belarus Free Theatre.

Instead of words I would like to leave a sheet of white paper. This is my dream of freedom now. This is how I understand the feeling of being free, inside and out.

Kiryl Kanstantsinau joined Belarus Free Theatre's drama school, Fortinbras, in February 2012. In April 2012, he was arrested along with the audience during a Belarus Free Theatre film screening.

When I was at drama school, I remember there being two different classes involving improvisation.

One was based on a very structured, analytical, rule-based form that developed out of the teachings of an American theatre practitioner named Uta Hagen.

The other was a rule-free, very fluid, anarchic form that had been developed out of the work of a British improv group called Theatre Machine. Two very different paths to unlocking creativity and exploring freedom from the constraints of a pre-existing text.

It was fascinating to see how we, as students, responded to these two confrontations with freedom and the possibilities inherent in entering the unknown.

The whole concept of improvisation seems to suggest utter freedom of imagination and infinite possibility in exploring what is spontaneous and of the moment. Yet, the most common result in both, very different classes, was a sort of leaden stultification and a parade of one empty cliché after another.

In the Uta Hagen 'method' class, the sheer weight of methodology and feeling of looming judgement if you strayed off the path of rigorous authenticity seemed to crush all spontaneity and rob the whole process of any joy or excitement.

Whereas, in the other, unstructured class with no rules and nothing to constrain our unfettered imaginations, we would just stand there, blinking in the dazzling light of total freedom, totally immobilized by the lack of any structure and groping for anything familiar to hang onto. This most often led to a terror-fueled clinging onto the most hackneyed and superficial of elements, like drowning bodies clutching at any passing piece of driftwood in a desperate attempt to stay afloat.

Very occasionally, in one class or the other, a glimmer of something vital and truly alive could thrillingly and seemingly out of nowhere suddenly come into being and the sheer exhilaration of possibility would momentarily electrify the room, but that was almost always the exception to the dull and lifeless rule.

What both classes shared was a tangible sense of fear. Not just the nervousness and anxiety that inevitably accompanies any kind of performance, especially one relying so much on the unknown.

This was different.

On the one hand, there was the terror of knowing that, in our desperate attempts to gain the favour of whichever priest or priestess of the 'method' orthodoxy we were being cruelly scrutinized by that day, we would inevitably break one or other of the endless, barely understood rules and that our transgressions would lead us to being shamed before our peers and punished for being an example of bourgeois fakery and vacuous superficiality. Judged as unworthy, traitorous and empty.

On the other, there was the almost existential terror of being granted that most precious of boons – utter and total freedom – and finding ourselves unworthy of it, unable to function in its munificent presence. When told we could do anything, we found we could do nothing. Like Icarus, the burning sun of total freedom turned our anticipated performing swoops and dives into a waxy formless mess and a plummeting awareness of our own failure as we descended into an ocean of chaos and vapidity. Structureless and unregulated, our most base of instincts would inevitably take control. Selfish, vulgar, infantile displays of power-grabs and status battles would play out, greedy and ugly and animalistic. Often violent and slapstick cruel. We were encouraged not to self-censor and for those observing not to judge. This primal crudity was necessary to purge through in order to get to the real creative gold that might lay beneath. Well, the veins were mighty hard to find but the journey was certainly instructive about what can happen when the shackles of regulation are removed.

Those two classes that I took almost twenty-five years ago now have remained with me. I am reminded of them whenever I come across any discussion of the concept of 'freedom'. And they are always useful in reminding me of some of the more surprising aspects of the realities of it, at least in my very limited and privileged experience of it.

Ex-President of the United States, Ronald Reagan, said 'Man is not free unless government is limited'. He advocated deregulation of the financial markets and allowing capitalism complete freedom to self-regulate society.

Nobel Prize-winning economist Alvin E Roth said, 'when we speak about a free market, we shouldn't be thinking of a free-for-all, but rather a market with well-designed rules that make it work for all'.

If I ever come across an improvisation class created by Roth, I'm signing up.

Michael Sheen is a Welsh actor. While performing *Hamlet* at the Young Vic Theatre in 2011, he took part in a reading for Belarus Free Theatre at the Serpentine Gallery.

VICTORIA BIRAN

Freedom is the possibility to act or make decisions according to one's beliefs of what is important, valuable and necessary. Freedom is not satisfying somebody else's expectations. I don't know how to achieve it. I'm on the way. I think self-contemplation and finding new ways to increase our self-consciousness could be helpful.

Victoria Biran studied at the Belarusian State University as a journalist and literary editor for four years, but was forced to interrupt her studies because of the reluctance of the university to accept her work with Belarus Free Theatre.

I think the best thing I can contribute to a book on freedom is information. The most useful information is to know how the Central Banks control the economy by creating debt. If you understand this you can work out how everything fits together, what's wrong and what we can do.

The central banks are private banks. The US Federal Bank is one, the Bank of England, another. They are organised by the Bank for International Settlements (BIS) in Zurich. These central banks print money. Today, they do this by pressing buttons. They create virtual money out of nothing. This money is loaned to other banks, monopolies and governments. It has now become a debt. The central banks prefer if it the loans are never paid because what they want is the interest – which accumulates out of all proportion to reality. This means they always have fantastic amounts of money to lend and they don't have to print virtual money except in an emergency. It also means that central banks come to own everything – because they own debt. How often have we heard of a poor country selling its assets and natural resources just to keep up with interest payments on the debt it has been forced to borrow?

The monopolies work this system for the central banks. They do the actual job of wrecking the planet and exploiting its people (cheap labour). They suck up small businesses.

My Politicians R CRIMINALS Campaign explains how politicians self-serve this political/ financial system.

#politiciansRcriminals: pro-profit, anti-people.

Dame Vivienne Westwood is a fashion designer and activist. She supports the work of Belarus Free Theatre and spoke on a platform discussion after their performance of *Trash Cuisine* at the Young Vic in 2013.

Total freedom is paralysis. Once we make a choice and commit ourselves to something, we are less free; but, crucially, we have EXERCISED our freedom.

We do not face the torment or the denial of freedom that people suffer in countries like Belarus. However, all too often we are denied the opportunity to EXERCISE our freedom. In a supposedly free, capitalist democracy we are told that competition increases our freedom of choice – in education, in health care, in the retail marketplace etc, but the reality is that this choice is not free at all. It is completely circumscribed and defined by class and wealth.

For me the most insidious and damaging instance of the loss of freedom of choice lies in the basic human right to express ourselves – most particularly when we are young – to realise our creative potential. Inside every individual is creativity waiting to be tapped, to be stimulated, to be expressed. It represents our very humanity.

All too often we are simply passive receivers of the arts. But nothing is more guaranteed to give us a sense of identity, self confidence and self esteem, than the opportunity to express ourselves. Such creativity is hardwired into our DNA. Any child will draw, paint, scribble, perform, dance, invent, imagine and play. Without inhibition or self-consciousness. But what happens to this impulse?

Our education system is failing lamentably. The government is not only cutting back on arts and humanities departments in higher education and forcibly removing the arts from the national curriculum, they are actively discouraging young people from studying the arts at all. The result is, we are breeding generations of young people who feel alienated, disenfranchised, frustrated and angry. We are neglecting, at our peril, the invisible part of the nation's health – our emotional, psychological and spiritual selves. This is very dangerous, but not entirely unexpected. Art provokes, asks uncomfortable questions, challenges received assumptions and refuses to accept black and white, whilst exploring infinite shades of grey. It points a light into the dim and distant corners of our lives and of our world.

I was recently smuggled into Belarus – the last dictatorship in Europe – to work underground in Minsk with Belarus Free Theatre on Shakespeare. Before we started, I asked each one what it was that, above all else, motivated them to put themselves at such considerable personal risk. They all, in their different ways, gave the same reply – an irresistible, fundamental human need to express themselves.

In this country we live in a 'free' democracy, and yet the vast majority of our young people are denied this human right. The imperative to communicate. We must protest at this denial of our children's freedom. We have to oppose the great god materialism and the siren call of commodity fetishism and insist that our culture is our birthright.

The marginalisation and trivialisation of the arts and the inadequacies of our education system are of course not as dreadful as the censorship and repression imposed by dictatorships such as in Belarus. It would be sentimental to claim they are. But, whilst actively campaigning against such regimes, we would do well to take a long hard look at ourselves and address this insidious, daily removal of freedom of choice here at home.

Michael Attenborough CBE has been Director of the Hampstead Theatre, Principal Associate Director of the RSC and most recently Artistic Director of the Almeida Theatre, where he gave Belarus Free Theatre one of their first key London residencies. He is now a Trustee of Belarus Free Theatre.

Never before have I felt so unfree as while writing '300 words about freedom'. Freedom as a category is so obvious that it requires constant refinements. After all, everyone constantly talk and dreams of 'freedom=happiness'. Perhaps that's the reason why it sells so well in modern day society. I wouldn't say that those categories are even present in my life, thus I question: 'Where do I feel the limitations on my freedom are?' I can in all honesty say – everywhere and nowhere. For example, no one ever asked me whether I wanted to appear in this world, to be born in the Soviet Union, in a family of miners, if I wanted this body type, this hair colour, or even these sexual preferences. No one asked me why years have passed for me to accept these things. It seems that at the age of forty I have found a harmonious balance and some might even feel that I handle myself well and am quite 'happy'. However, I know that in front of me awaits some fatal non-freedoms: aging and

Vaclav Havel – photographer unknown

Underground performance – © Georgie Weedon

Police raid of Belarus performance © Svetlana Sugako

In rehearsal for *Price of Money* – © Georgie Weedon

merry christmas, Ms Meadows, performed in Belarus © Svetlana Sugako

Natalia and Ai Weiwei marching in solidarity with refugees, London, September 2015
© Natalia Kaliada

Belarus Not Found © Georgie Weedon

Give A Body Back protest, New York, 2015 © Georgie Weedon

Made in USSR © Georgie Weedon

Price of Money © Nicolai Khalezin

Minsk, 2011: A Reply to Kathy Acker, performed in Belarus © Svetlana Sugako

Being Harold Pinter © Nicolai Khalezin

Trash Cuisine © Nicolai Khalezin

Fringe First award, Edinburgh, 2011 – photographer unknown

dying. Thus what kind of 'freedom' are we even talking about?

When the conversation touches upon society, the question of political and social freedoms in that society arises. According to this, a so-called 'index of happiness' is formed to judge any social group. Nevertheless, any law to some degree is a limitation on someone's freedom. Limitation for the better, in order to find harmonious social cohesion. 'Better', which sometimes develops into censorship even in the most progressive countries. And when this balance is seriously disturbed, dictatorships such as the Soviet Union or modern day Belarus, where I was lucky enough to live in, arise.

One of the great minds once said that you could be free even in prison. In fact, I know a lot of artistic people in Belarus who feel absolutely free, as in their words: 'no one forbids them from doing anything, thus they say and do whatever they desire'. Yet, for some reason they say and do only what is allowed. Or rather, not forbidden. Maybe this is happiness. Regardless, they give the impression of rather happy people.

I was fortunate to a small degree: neither in my personal life, nor in my art, did I get that link with authority or those possessing it. Therefore, I just didn't have a choice. Or rather, the choice was always there. To be or not to be, you don't get a third option. Just once I found an endless reservoir of black fear in myself, although I can't say I was afraid of any one thing in that moment.

I don't know what freedom is; yet I certainly know what lack of it means. Non-freedom is fear. Fear to accept yourself, fear not to be accepted by others (and I'm not certain which fear is greater). According to this you get the fear to touch whom you desire, fear to say what you think, fear to do what you want. Fear that paralyses you, enters your dreams and eats your soul.

So, then came the moment when I just physically felt, either I begin to rid myself of the fear of this particular moment, or it will engulf me. Perhaps the process of overcoming the fear/unfreedom is freedom/happiness. In this case, freedom is something you have to fight for everyday. After all, you have to be on guard, as your lack of freedom easily changes its appearance. Today it's an external enemy (the rulers, the dictators, the censor); tomorrow it's you, your friends, self-censorship and conformism.

However, we shouldn't be afraid of obtaining fear. For fear closely intertwines our private and public selves, it shines a light on the shadowy areas of any society. Moreover, fear is the best landmark of work and life. To be more precise, the landmark is the overcoming of this fear.

The only thing I would like to get rid of once and for all, are the nightmares where I see myself before I found the reservoir of fear and thus try my best in order to pretend to appear happy and free.

Vladimir Shcherban is an original partner of Belarus Free Theatre and joined the company shortly after it was founded in 2005, introducing actors who became the foundation for the existing permanent ensemble. In 2008, he also helped Natalia Kaliada and Nicolai Khalezin found Fortinbras, the only underground arts school in Belarus.

In my opinion, each individual limits freedom. They limit it by letting their own rights be infringed. It starts with something small, even imperceptible, like the cancellation of their benefits, and if they allow this to pass unchallenged and decide to suffer through it, then it can end up changing them completely. Worse than all of this is the fact that nothing really changes. People adjust and get used to the recent alterations to their life. In the place of freedom comes fear, fear you have done something that is forbidden. Fear of creating something new (what if it is unlawful?), fear of being different (what if you are punished for it?). Fear that things can get worse. Fear of everything...

And what is truly scary, is that people start being afraid of things that don't exist, limiting their personal freedom to a minimum.

If you ask me, you need to find freedom in your mind. To realise you are not free, and start to remove the barriers one by one.

Maryna Yakubovich joined Belarus Free Theatre in 2006. She was dismissed from the Belarusian Army Theatre in 2008 for co-operating with the company.

In Britain, our Human Rights Act (HRA) – which enshrines the European Convention on Human Rights into UK law – has become the political punchbag of choice. But it's my experience that we all believe in the fundamental freedoms it protects – as long as they're our own, or those of 'people like us'. It's when they apply to 'others' that problems arise.

The principle of equal treatment under the law provides the solution. Aspiring to be a tolerant, compassionate, equal nation is all very laudable – but it counts for nothing if those values aren't enforceable in law. There have been times in Europe's not-too-distant past when minority groups have struggled to receive the same recognition as the majority; when vulnerable individuals have been deprived of the support and protection to let them live with dignity; when states has been left seemingly unaccountable for grossly illegitimate uses of power. In recent years, when we've collectively failed to respect and protect each other, the Convention and – in the UK – our HRA has let us make amends, rendering our rights a reality, not just an aspiration. They've proven our most effective tools for holding the powerful to account and challenging state abuse, neglect and mistreatment.

This year, the UK's great and good have lined up to celebrate the 800th anniversary of Magna Carta – that early, tentative step toward equal treatment under the law and curtailing executive power. For all the patriotic gusto it inspires, the great charter is an unenforceable relic. It cannot help ordinary people keep the state in check. But it set us on the path to our modern Bill of Rights: the meaningful protection of the HRA.

It's a dark irony that many of the same people so keen to wrap themselves in Magna Carta are so blindly intent on undermining its objective by repealing our HRA. The scant proposals we've seen for its replacement – the 'British Bill of Rights' – would give the politicians unprecedented powers to pick and choose which and whose rights matter most, carving out exceptions to the reach of human rights law for certain groups. They may even see us withdraw from the Convention – sending a terrible message to tyrants in Europe and further afield.

And, beneath the barrage of aggressive misinformation, that's the critics' real problem with the Convention: it protects everybody. That means people who have committed crimes, that means foreigners, that means both the 'hard-working families' and 'scroungers' that the UK's politicians and press seem so keen to pit against each other – and that means me, you and yours.

Fundamental rights are universal and even-handed. They weren't designed to make the powerful comfortable, win votes, or make it easy to push through illiberal policies – they were designed to keep us free. The Convention was our continent's answer to the horrors of the Holocaust – our pledge that rights would never again be limited based on skin colour, nationality, sex, religion, political opinion or any other arbitrary status.

The greatest threat to our freedom is that we sign it away, thinking it's only those 'others' who'll lose out. We can be so obsessed with perceived threats to our freedoms from outside our community that we forget how easily we undermine them from within. But the easiest way to drive a coach and horses through freedoms for which previous generations paid an astronomical price is to say they won't be for everyone.

The world is shrinking and ever more interconnected. We have to decide whether to seek protection as human beings everywhere or live with the vulnerability of being foreigners in every country other than our own. I know which I choose – and in which direction I want my country to lead.

A barrister by background, Shami Chakrabarti has been Director of Liberty (The National Council for Civil Liberties) since September 2003 and has written, spoken and broadcast widely on the importance of the post-World War 2 human rights framework as an essential component of democratic society. Shami was introduced to Belarus Free Theatre by Maria Miller MP, the former Culture Secretary and a great friend of the theatre.

Chekhov, who was never keen to align himself with any particular movement, said that his only political determination was to live a life 'free from lies and free from violence'. I have always found that to be pretty unbeatable. Where we find ourselves mired in either untruth or physical oppression, whether it is the transparent and hideous brutality of some regimes, or the less palpable and more insidious constrictions of the capitalist west, we should assume the right, and hope to have the courage, to speak out against such lies or violence.

Everyone should be allowed to live the life that they choose to live, as long as it neither hurts nor harms others. Where we find ourselves in the relatively lucky position that we enjoy a substantial degree of freedom, it is our duty to protect those freedoms rigorously, and to ensure that they are ever further spread out to any and to all. For who should be happy if not everyone?

It is also our duty to enjoy those freedoms, to celebrate them, to party and be happy.

However reckless or frivolous such enjoyment might seem, it is nothing to be ashamed of, and I suspect that the world is more keen to gravitate towards joy than towards misery. Making theatre is sometimes a hard business, and often a grave business, but it is also full of pleasure, and we should not hide such pleasures away because we feel a censor of seriousness sitting over our shoulders, and telling us that we should look glum.

There are many inhibitions placed in front of being free in the theatre, some by others and some by ourselves. It is our privilege and our right and our duty, to burst through those and to say in the face of the many who will always say 'why?', a resounding and free 'why not?'.

Dominic Dromgoole is the Artistic Director of Shakespeare's Globe in London. In 2012 Belarus Free Theatre performed *King Lear* as part of their 'Globe to Globe' Festival.

Ice in the prison courtyard

Freedom?... Well, now I certainly know what it is. Freedom is lying on the icy ground of the prison yard dying of laughter. It is true, pure and accessible freedom. Trust me.

I remember very clearly how I came to understand and feel it. I was sitting in a KGB jail accused of organising a mass disorder, which meant I could be sentenced to between five and fifteen years of jail. Sitting in the neighbouring cells were my husband and our friends, all of us having been declared a large criminal group. A special unit of masked men were deployed in the prison especially for us. Even the prison guards obeyed these men. They had no faces, they never took off their masks. We were completely at the mercy of these monsters. Their goal was to intimidate, threaten and torture. We women refused to take the daily hour-long walks we were allowed, so essential in prison, just to avoid running into those bastards.

And yet I understood that I was free. Free from their authority, from the prison walls, from the fear of spending fifteen years in jail. So, this is how it happened. I was led to an interrogation room. To get there, inmates are taken through the inner courtyard into the main KGB building. To access the courtyard you need to open a massive door next to the last cell. This is done by the guards. When I was led out our prison guards were chatting amongst themselves near the door. I was lost in my thoughts and, completely forgetting that they were the ones who should open the door, I tried to open it myself. But I got the wrong door and attempted to break into cell number 18. The guards laughed, finding it so funny they didn't even try to stop me. Then one of the bastards in a mask arrived. He was nicknamed 'Kadyrov', and was supposed to escort me. We distinguished who was who by their voices, Kadyrov being the vilest of all the faceless men. The guards immediately fell silent, Kadyrov opened the door that led to the backyard, and as he did I began to shake with laughter. I realised that I was trying to break into someone's cell and just like the guards moments ago I doubled over. Kadyrov screamed, 'No laughter!' And then that strange part of the human mind kicked in. If ordered not to scratch your nose under any circumstances, your nose would no doubt start itching as if a hoard of mosquitoes had just landed on it. If someone orders you to stop thinking of green elephants, well then green elephants are going to stampede through your mind. And if we are commanded to stop laughing, there is nothing on Earth that can make us stop.

Kadyrov screamed once again, 'Didn't I just order you to stop laughing?!' By this time we were already in the prison yard. I tried to supress my laughter, gurgling, spraying and squealing in my attempts to stop, but then I slipped on the icy path and fell down. And that's the moment I burst. I laughed out loud and at that moment there was nothing in the world that could've stopped me, not batons, nor stun guns. I had a fifteen-year sentence and Kadyrov hanging over me, but I could not stop. I writhed with laughter on the dirty, icy footpath in the prison yard and strangely enough I felt almost happy. And most importantly, free.

If your laughter only begins or ends by someone's order then you are a slave, an eternal prisoner. But if they can't control your laughter, you are free.

Irina Khalip is a Belarusian journalist, human rights defender and former political prisoner. She was arrested together with her husband, presidential candidate Andrei Sannikov, on 19 December 2010 and they were charged as organizers of mass disorders. Irina is the winner of European Hero Prize in the category 'Brave Heart' (Time Europe magazine, UK) in 2005, Hermann Kesten Prize (Germany) in 2012, PEN-Pinter Prize (Great Britain) in 2013. Irina says 'I am friends with Belarus Free Theatre and we all desperately love freedom.'

I am often asked what my preferred definition of forgiveness is and as the years go by increasingly I struggle to come up with an adequate answer. I used to quote Mark Twain's: 'Forgiveness is the fragrance that the violet sheds on the heel that crushed it,' because I like the way this shows forgiveness to be messy but potentially healing. However now, eleven years on, when I'm asked to define forgiveness I just choose one word, the single concept – 'freedom'.

Wilma Derksen's story is one of many examples of how forgiveness liberates. I met Wilma and her husband Cliff in Winnipeg in 2013 when she told me how in 1984 their thirteen-year-old daughter, Candace, disappeared on her way home from school. Six weeks later, on the same day Candace's body was discovered, a stranger knocked at their door saying he was the parent of a murdered child too. He then proceeded to describe everything he'd lost – his health, his relationships, his concentration; he'd even lost all memory of his daughter because now he could only think of the trauma and hate that followed.

Wilma told me – 'We went to bed that night horrified by the graphic picture this father had painted. Having just been through the pain of losing our daughter, it now seemed we might lose everything else as well. And so we made a decision that night that we would respond differently, and we chose the path of forgiveness.'

Wilma's story shows that forgiveness is not a linear journey, nor a quick fix cure-all, but fluid and ever-changing. Over the subsequent decades she describes how 'forgiveness would prod me, guide me, heal me, label me, enlighten me, imprison me, free me and in the end define me.' Her story also shows how the personal freedom that forgiveness affords can alienate others. In Wilma's case some of her community accused her of not loving Candace because she forgave. Others said forgiveness was dangerous because it promoted a society where all murderers go free. In some similar stories shared through The Forgiveness Project those who forgive are accused by family members of stampeding on the memory of their loved ones.

Forgiveness is threatening because it can set one victim against another. For instance Eva Kor, a survivor of Auschwitz and medical experiments performed by Dr Josef Mengele, has been called a traitor by some fellow survivors for declaring that if you don't forgive you'll be locked into the prison of victimhood.

While I know how liberating it is to forgive (because trauma identifies the person with the deed and can freeze relationships and life stories forever) when forgiveness is promoted as a duty or an obligation, or if the rhetoric of forgiveness is used by politicians to avoid accountability, then it can become harmful. Forgiveness must always be a personal choice, only then will personal testimonies demonstrating peaceful solutions to conflict be able to mend fractured communities. As Nelson Mandela wrote: 'As I walked out the door toward the gate that would lead to my freedom, I knew if I didn't leave my bitterness and hatred behind, I'd still be in prison.'

Marina Cantacuzino is the founder of The Forgiveness Project which in 2015 was a partner organisation for BFT's platform discussion after the performance of *Discover Love*

I'm not sure I'm at all the right person to write anything about individual perspective and personal experience regarding freedom – I am Canadian. Sure I am Chinese by blood, and was born and raised in the Philippines, but I've been in Canada since the age of eleven, and can imagine no other personal cultural identity than Canadian, with the privileges which accompany that. I am also a lawyer, in addition to being a theatre producer. So I recognize that the freedom I am privileged to live with, is among the widest and greatest in the world. I have a certain amount of economic freedom, and then I have the freedoms guaranteed under Canada's Charter of Rights and Freedoms, including the fundamental freedoms of conscience and religion; of thought, belief, opinion and expression, including freedom of the press and other media of communication; of peaceful assembly; and of association. The Charter guarantees further freedoms in democratic rights, mobility rights, legal rights and equality rights.

And yet… our Canadian freedoms are by no means absolute. They are subject to 'reasonable limits' as can be 'demonstrably justified in a free and democratic society'. And the last nine years under the current government – the 'Harper Government' as it has rebranded, instead of 'Government of Canada' – has given real cause to fear for the (further) erosion of freedoms. With Canada currently in a campaign towards the next Federal election on 19 October 2015, the greatest current challenge to Canadian freedoms may lie with the results of the ballot box. In the last two weeks, both the *New York Times* and the (UK) *Guardian* have published harsh criticism of the Harper government, echoing what many journalists, academics, artists and other Canadians have been declaiming for years. Sadly the greatest challenge to Canadian freedom may be within its own borders, with its own elected government.

The election of a new Federal government is certainly not the sole solution, but would definitely go a long way to righting the path towards the precious fundamental freedoms that we must never take for granted and that make Canada one of the best places in the world to live, and the only country that I would currently choose to make my home.

Derrick Chua is an entertainment lawyer and independent theatre producer based in Toronto, Canada. He came to know of Belarus Free Theatre after seeing *Trash Cuisine* at the Edinburgh Fringe and then spending over an hour talking about the show and company with Natalia Kaliada, standing outside a pub in Edinburgh.

Poor legislation is what restricts freedom. I am totally convinced of it from personal experience. The authorities, the legislature, don't always act as they are supposed to. They are careless and often too bored to resolve your issues. And because of this carelessness and boredom, mistakes take place, people lose their freedom. Belarus's legal system is simply paradoxical. Take the recent 'social parasite' Law which states that every able-bodied person in Belarus has a duty to work and help build a utopian communist society. It is an absolutely mind-blowing restriction of freedom! Not allowing a person to be un-employed is basically the same as making them a slave.

But there is also another form of restriction, one that is inside us. For me it is sloth. Whenever I am occupied with something, I am free, yet if I stop the shackles of sloth appear on my feet, arms and thoughts. It's a terrible state of non-freedom; the feeling that you are trapped by an unknown species, neither fish nor flesh. Again it is this indifference which generates everything, even unjust laws.

When I struggle with these shackles, I begin by freeing my arms and feet: they are easier to free than the head, then I just start walking. This is my salvation.

Andrei Urazau has been studying in the Fortinbras laboratory of Belarus Free Theatre since February 2012. He graduated to the permanent ensemble in December of that year and has sinced performed in several Belarus Free Theatre productions.

Freedom in the modern world is becoming intrinsically linked to the digital world. Even without possession of an electronic device, it's becoming virtually impossible to prevent leaving a revealing digital trail. From biometrics, CCTV, smart meters and banking a cascade of data is being generated on us all that has the very real potential to betray us. This form of subtle surveillance can easily be turned against the citizenry to facilitate oppression in the physical world, as historical lessons show. Freedom to choose who knows what about you is the essence of privacy and is under unprecedented threat.

The revelations of Edward Snowden and whistleblowers from other countries have given us a glimpse into the extensive efforts of states to keep the world under constant watch. We have seen everything from charities, lawyers, the UN, companies and even entire countries being unlawfully monitored from remote locations to control and influence their leaders and populations. Such nations cannot be free under constant surveillance. In particular, journalists cannot communicate secretly with whistleblowers to reveal unlawful activities of the powerful elites. It is vital that the artistic community plays one of its long-standing roles in highlighting these threats to freedom in a succinct and emotive way for the general public.

However, there are some positive developments in the technical and legal fields emerging. Laws on surveillance are now under review or being debated around the world. It is possible that they may lead to meaningful oversight and legal safeguards that are transparent. Unfortunately, such laws often distinguish between citizens and foreigners and therefore activities outside a nation's borders are unregulated with no accountability. Technology might be able to fill gaps, including this, left in the legal landscape.

Technological developments however do not make such distinctions and in particular open source and free software can be universally downloaded and deployed. Encryption, The Onion Router (TOR), Virtual Private Networks (VPNs) and Off the Record (OTR) Chat are increasing in sophistication and uptake. Using such solutions, individuals can be empowered to communicate with more security and be free to be themselves. The free flow of ideas, even ones politically unpopular, can spread as intended and a level of democratic debate can take place even in the face of constant monitoring from regimes.

We are seeing efforts to undermine these advances. States are bribing scientists and companies to employ vulnerable software and encryption so that security is removed. States that once derided other states for hacking have now been exposed as using this tactic routinely. It is vital that our freedom to communicate safely is encouraged by governments through their laws and policies. It is also vital that we keep pressure on them to value security as a primary goal as our world becomes increasingly digital. We must be allowed to protect our data from abuse by third parties – our freedom depends on it.

Dr Richard Tynan is the Technologist at Privacy International. He works on surveillance issues and how our modern world is threatening the right to privacy.
He assisted Belarus Free Theatre during a period of time when their website was attacked. Coincidentally, this attack occurred as their play opened in New York.

When I hear the word 'freedom' I involuntarily recall the characteristic revealed by Vladimir Pozner in one of his recent TV shows *'England in General and in Particular'*. In one of the episodes Pozner asked the same question to Britons and refugees, asking them how they felt about the growing numbers of immigrants in the United Kingdom. Both groups answered in a similar way: 'It's very good, we are happy about this.' But later on the bravest ones admitted that, in all honesty, if there weren't cameras present they would have said something completely different. Yet the possibility of judgment and punishment, as the country has strong democratic views, stopped them from saying anything. What surprised me most about this was that the refugees who were unaware of the cameras reacted even more negatively than the native Britons.

I believe that our country acts as a mirror to the UK, even though the GDP, mentality and culture are in complete opposition, because questions of this type answered on camera make people answer in a way that they won't be judged upon.

For me, 'limitations of freedom' is a rather abstract phrase, maybe because until now I wasn't able to relate to it. However I asked someone who was serving a lengthy jail sentence for committing a serious crime and he said: 'When you are not free all your dreams, your thoughts and desires construct and aim to one large and distant, yet very specific goal, to free yourself from this bondage of captivity. For you in your cell, freedom seems to be the only vital yet unreachable thing on Earth. However, the moment you have it, it loses all importance, as you don't have this all-encompassing desire to own it any longer. You appreciate it, of course, but you don't take it seriously. Freedom becomes something casual, and natural. Only you can limit your own freedom, mainly by being afraid to take the wrong step.'

Without freedom everything changes to some extent, yet at the same time nothing changes at all.

Freedom is something that each individual can obtain only by himself and then he has to decide what to do with it.

Yuliya Shauchuk is a member of Belarus Free Theatre's permanent ensemble. She lost her job at the National Theatre of Belarusian Drama in 2011 for participating in an interview in the 'free news'.

The most widely sought freedom is freedom from doubt, which is why such huge numbers have accepted obedience to an authority that tells them what to believe. But the price is conflict with those who do not share their certainties.

The very opposite kind of freedom, for all individuals to be able to say what they please, also has a snag; the likelihood that no one may listen. Seizing power from dictatorial governments has a snag too, because however well meaning the victors are, power corrupts, and besides, private tyrannies remain and can be as oppressive as public ones.

There are many more freedoms that neither ideology nor law can assure: freedom from illusions about others and about oneself, freedom from prejudices, obsessive habits and greed, freedom from loneliness, freedom of the imagination, freedom from self-censorship, shyness and a narrow mind, which can be as constraining as official censorship, freedom from being a victim of the war of the sexes, freedom from the limitations and stress that a career path imposes.

I have searched for these intimate freedoms by developing a new way of remembering the past and imagining the future. My first aim is to avoid the worse kind of imprisonment, a life spent repeating the mistakes that previous generations have made. Instead of dreaming up a utopia, I use biographies from previous centuries as instruments to provoke imaginations, and to explore what can be achieved by new kinds of relationships, not just between couples who live together or fall in and out of love, but also by couples of the mind, who independently of physical union, time or place, and untrammelled by possessiveness, intermingle their memories and thoughts.

Whereas the height of freedom today is individual creativity, based on the example of the solitary geniuses of the past, I have invited dissimilar people to discover one another more profoundly through new kinds of conversation, one-to-one, so as to expand their horizons by interacting across the barriers of nation, religion and wealth. To be free implies feeling fully alive, rather than 20% or 50% alive, which is often the result of soul-destroying work. So we start practical experiments in different occupations to discover how work can make the enhancement of each person's existence a priority.

Humans are not born free. No one enters the world without fear. The most elusive of all freedoms is freedom from fear. The best route out of fear is curiosity, which dissolves problems into microscopic particles, each of which becomes an object of wonder rather than a threat. Cultivating a wide curiosity about everything that humans have tried, succeeded and failed to do, wherever and whenever they have lived, breeds both humility and courage. Freedom requires courage in many different domains.

Theodore Zeldin's books include *A History of French Passions*, *An Intimate History of Humanity* and *The Hidden Pleasures of Life*. Belarus Free Theatre published a film of him talking about his ideas on the Ministry of Counterculture website.

I've been to Minsk and saw *Time of Women*, a Belarus Free Theatre performance, there in secret. Two of the women the play was based on were sitting with us in the tiny audience crammed into a studio flat.

I understand the comparative luxury we have in the UK of having the freedom to express any dissenting views, the freedom to protest, the freedom to challenge power. But with all that apparent freedom, the British sink further and further into a neoliberalist nightmare of terminal consumerism, blind xenophobia, fetid individualism; a world where the selfie-stick is king and people recognise Beyoncé but not the Prime Minister.

While the government relentlessly attack the poor, the vulnerable and the disabled, despite all our freedom to dissent and protest, less people come on an action than could fit in that studio flat in Minsk.

Which oppression is greater between Belarus and the UK? Where they have the KGB, we have a failure of solidarity, a disengagement from caring about anything other than our own self. Where they have state controlled media, we have a media owned by a handful of right wing billionaires. State-controlled apathy, in both nations, is actualised to perfection. We all learn to play the fiddle as our world burns.

The greater horror is not mass civil disobedience; the greatest horror is mass civil obedience. What happened to us? What happened to all the Belarusians who know that Lukashenko is a tyrant and a monster but still remain quiet and compliant, in effect, condoning his absurd vanity and cruelty? What happened to all the British who know that austerity is a scam to benefit the 1%, that the banks caused the crisis yet still dole out billions in bonuses while a million need food banks to survive, that our Prime Minister and his pals are inordinately privileged, arrogant posh boys playing their part in growing an all powerful plutocracy that mocks the last ragged bones of democracy? Where is everyone? In a country where the KGB won't disappear you, why are the British so obedient? So reluctant to stand up and be counted and defy this absurd, murderous kleptocracy?

Having the freedom to dissent is not enough. It is only valuable to those who retain a connection with their humanity. We have become an atomised nation where nobody knows their neighbours anymore; fear reigns and greed is exalted.

Young people are growing up not even knowing that the choice to challenge assumptions, to fight back against injustice and join the struggle to create a fairer world, exists.

There's the horror. The extinction of hope. The daily misery of poverty, gross inequality, cruelty, fear and injustice becomes the unquestioned norm. Freedom becomes a word more associated with adverts for jeans or tampons than fighting for any other possible futures than the one our apathy condemns us to.

Stéphane Hessel was right; our only chance is a revolution in morals, a revolution in the answer to the question 'what did we come here for anyway?'

It is mass civil obedience that is the problem. We need to reclaim the word freedom and remind our youth that part of being human is to fight for justice for all. It is a beautiful species, capable of immense achievements but is about to drown itself in its own apathy and fear. We are sitting in front of a violin and banging on it with spoons. All power to those few who are beginning to pick it up and play.

Now more than ever we need Belarus Free Theatre, as we need the next Occupy. Will it grow in the streets of Paris over the 2015 Climate Change Conference where hundreds of thousands of young people are massing to take back the chance to write their own history again? Will it grow in the US with #blacklivesmatter? Will it grow in you as you return to that question and ask yourself 'what did we come here for anyway?' As the current failure of our leaders and the corporations, banks and industrial military complex that own them, is becoming horribly apparent, it is rapidly becoming clear to us all what we didn't come here for. It is up to you to use your freedom to fight for something better than this. The cavalry are not coming; there is no rescuing knight. Only you. Now. Being alive before you die. Only you.

Jamie Kelsey-Fry is a teacher, writer and activist. He connected Belarus Free Theatre to grassroots activism in the UK and as an educational consultant.

You need to finish what you've started. Don't worry about me. I defended my family from those jerks in uniforms. You know me. I was a marine. Love you all.

That was the last phone conversation that I had with my father-in-law. His name was Nicolai. The next day he was dead.

The day before our last conversation the KGB, in search of my husband and I, raided his apartment in Minsk. We had already been named 'Enemies of the State' by the Belarusian regime.

In the best case scenario our friends are refugees, as we are. In the worst case, they are imprisoned, tortured, poisoned, kidnapped or killed. Our native language is prohibited. The regime eats our country from within, destroying families, culture and traditions. One of our friends said that she only feels free and becomes herself when she leaves Belarus.

When I shared that story with the aboriginal people of the Northern Territory in

Darwin, Australia, they said that this is exactly what they have endured, but for over 200 years.

The difference is that they are stronger than us.

They don't leave their country. They want to die where they are born.

There are basic things that my family, like many other families in my country, taught their children. These values are shared by the native people of Australia, who know about freedom in all its beauty when you have it; and in all its horror when it's taken from you. You are free when your family is with you and not torn apart, when you are able to walk on your land and feel safe, speak your language, experience your culture and traditions, and share food with strangers around a table knowing that they will not storm your house and keep you as prisoners in your own home.

In Aboriginal families grandparents teach their grandchildren how to live a life full of honour and dignity. How to be free, even when there is no freedom left.

We were smuggled out of our country. We thought if we applied external pressure on the government it would perhaps help our friends be released from prison. The strength of their spirit has helped them to stay free even when they are jailed. We may have physically escaped from our prison cells, but we can never be free until our friends are with us. With every single person who gets out of jail we move closer to finding that freedom.

But today people are still imprisoned in Belarus.

That last phone conversation with my father-in-law made our beliefs even stronger Most importantly, with that short speech full of love, passion, and courage, he set his son and me free.

After we were smuggled out of Belarus my own father lost his voice. The only thing left for him was to whisper, but it was enough to keep us moving.

Even though my father lost his voice I know that as long as he has the strength to whisper, my daughters have a chance to know what freedom truly means.

Natalia Kaliada is the founding co-Artistic Director of Belarus Free Theatre as well as a writer, producer and one of the most outspoken critics of Belarus's repressive regime. She has organised some hugely successful artistic human rights campaigns, including the Give A Body Back campaign. She is the co-creator, together with Nicolai Khalezin and Vladimir Shcherban, of Fortinbras, the only free theatre laboratory in Belarus.

Life is good – for some. For too many more it is impossible to look ahead, to conceive of another future, to walk with the sun on your face and with the wind at your back because feet are heavy, shoulders are weighed down, backs are bent and eyes flutter fearfully to see who is watching and what is holding you back.

How far could I walk for freedom? How many children could I embrace and wrap in a blanket of protection? How loud could I scream to make sure that my voice could be heard and unite with others in their cry for freedom?

Freedom violently torn away or maliciously, furtively, surreptitiously eroded. Freedom to read, to write, to think, to dance, to create, to sing – how far could I go?

Freedom to love, freedom to make a home, freedom not to hide – how hard would I fight?

Freedom to think, freedom to believe, freedom to dream, freedom to share, freedom to care.

Humanity has never ceased to wreak horror on one another – horrors we once thought were of another time, another world. But our time is now and our small world is becoming smaller with every breath we take. We can no longer sit back in our content and comfort, without taking responsibility, without acknowledging that we too are complicit.

Freedom to act, freedom to make visible what others try to hide. Freedom to take responsibility. Freedom to speak out when others cannot. Freedom to lift up those bent down, freedom to shout where others have been silenced.

Was there ever a 'free world' and another parallel one in chains? We are one world and if we do not use our freedom to free others, are we really free? Are we not equally enslaved, just by other masters? Masters that live within us, that limit us. The master that says: your life is good, it is not your problem. The master of contentment and complacency that keeps us silent.

The voices of artists, poets, dancers, musicians are the voices of change, the voices of defiance, the voices of courage, giving shape to thoughts that others cannot articulate. The voices that challenge, the voices that empower and unite. It is not an easy road, it can be a lonely road, but it is the only road – to use our freedom to free others – to walk with them, to lift them up, shout out for them, and to bring their dance and their song to the world.

Katherine Watson moved from Canada to join the European Cultural Foundation (ECF) in 2006 and has been Director since 2010. ECF has been a friend and supporter of Belarus Free Theatre since its early days and is honoured to have commissioned *Trash Cuisine* that premiered in the Stadsshouwburg Amsterdam in October 2012, in the context of ECF's programme, *Imagining Europe*.

'With freedom…comes responsibility.'

Ai Weiwei

TEN YEARS OF BELARUS FREE THEATRE

Often referred to as 'the last dictatorship in Europe', Belarus has remained in the grip of Alexander Lukashenko's administration since 1994. It is ranked 157th out of 180 countries for press and media freedom, designated as 'not free' by Freedom House and as 'repressed' by the Index of Economic Freedom. The last twenty-one years has seen the continued implementation of the death penalty, the bodies of the executed never released to their families, the kidnappings and murders of main opponents to the regime, the repeated imprisonment and intimidation of dissident voices, electoral candidates and pro-democracy activists and a profound lack of electoral transparency and legitimacy.

There are twenty-eight theatre companies in Belarus, twenty-seven of which are owned and run by the state; the other is Belarus Free Theatre.

On 30 March 2005, Natalia Kaliada, a diplomat and human rights campaigner, and Nicolai Khalezin, a newspaper editor, journalist and playwright, founded Belarus Free Theatre in Minsk. Theatre director Vladimir Shcherban joined them shortly after and introduced the actors that would become the foundation for their permanent ensemble. Together they established the company, creating a space for theatre and arts, free expression, enquiry, debate and education, a space to oppose and think through the consequences of living under a dictatorial regime.

Between 2005 and 2010 Belarus Free Theatre made over thirty shows and toured internationally to over thirty countries in five continents around the world. In Belarus the company have been banned and blacklisted, its Artistic Directors declared 'enemies of the state'. Alongside the producing of new work, and relentless performing at home and abroad, the company established the 'Fortinbras Theatre Laboratory', an intensive and entirely free education programme in Belarus focused on the relationship between independent arts practice, internationalism and social justice. To date, over sixty young Belarusians have completed the programme at great personal risk, a number going on to join the company's permanent ensemble.

Since 2013, when BFT's landlord was forced to evict the company due to repeated threats, the company performs and teaches in the woodland, apartments, warehouses across the city. Despite regular police raids and detention of both the actors and audiences, over 30,000 people have seen performances and participated in after-show discussions in Belarus. Every one of these events has been free – in both senses of the word.

Rigged presidential elections in the winter of 2010 saw mass protest in Minsk. After violent clashes with state security services, over 2000 demonstrators were arrested and interned. Natalia Kaliada was released from jail swiftly due to a fortunate case of mistaken identity. Nicolai Khalezin went into hiding and on the run. Both were smuggled out of the country and headed to New York to perform with the rest of the company, before realizing that for their own safety there was no way they could go back. The vast majority of their friends and collaborators remained incarcerated for weeks, months, and in some cases years.

In June 2011 the British government granted Kaliada, Khalezin, Shcherban and actor Aleh Sidorchyk political asylum, and London's Young Vic theatre made the company Associate Artists, providing them with a 'home' and UK base. Falmouth University gave them the space for residencies where they could create new shows, not over Skype, but face to face with their actors and students.

Since then the company have continued their work in London and Minsk, where most of the company's actors and producers are still based, directing and teaching (often via Skype) and organizing teaching residencies for academics and artists from across the world. The company still performs weekly in Belarus and classes still take place every day. Shows continue to be raided and artists and audiences intimidated and detained.

Since 2011 six new shows have been made for international touring, to great critical acclaim, and associated high-impact human rights campaigns have been launched. The company's work has been acknowledged through awards including the Atlantic Council Freedom Award, the Freedom to Create Prize and the French Republic Award for Human Rights.

Over the last five years BFT has become increasingly recognized as a global movement, committed to the arts, internationalism and social justice through its producing, education and campaign programmes. BFT are now considered to be one of the most effective and internationally visible, arts-based, democracy initiatives in the world.

2015 marks ten years since Belarus Free Theatre was first created in Minsk as a platform for free expression through the arts. To mark this anniversary the company launched Staging a Revolution, a retrospective festival co-produced with the Young Vic in London and live streamed around the world.

With this book Belarus Free Theatre want to explore our changing ideas of freedom with the people who have met and worked with the company over the last ten years. Each piece gives an insight into what freedom means in the 21st century and the mixed emotions of joy, frustration and responsibility that come with it.

The result is a powerful, international collection of voices that encourage us to stand up for our liberties, and to fight oppression and censorship wherever it is.

You can find out more about Belarus Free Theatre and sign up to their newsletter at their website **www.belarusfreetheatre.com**.

Visit the Ministry of Counterculture, Belarus Free Theatre's news and media website, for interviews and insights into the arts and social change **www.moc.media/en**.

@bfreetheatre
#StagingaRevolution

First published in 2015 by Oberon Books Ltd
521 Caledonian Road, London N7 9RH
Tel: +44 (0) 20 7607 3637
Fax: +44 (0) 20 7607 3629
e-mail: info@oberonbooks.com
www.oberonbooks.com

A catalogue record for this book is available from the British Library.

HB ISBN: 9781783199877
E ISBN: 9781783199884

Cover design by Ai Weiwei

Printed, bound and converted by CPI Group (UK) Ltd, Croydon, CR0 4YY.

Visit www.oberonbooks.com to read more about all our books and to buy them. You will also find features, author interviews and news of any author events, and you can sign up for e-newsletters so that you're always first to hear about our new releases.